Alexander Finds a Home

by Vicky Ann Meier

Published 2024

Printed in the United States of America

First Edition
ISBN (softcover): 978-1-963380-13-2
ISBN (hardcover): 978-1-963380-14-9
ISBN (e-book): 978-1-963380-15-6

For information, address:
Holzer Books LLC
8 The Green, Ste. A
Dover, Delaware 19901 USA

For information about special discounts available for bulk purchases, sales promotions, and educational needs, contact: info@holzerbooksllc.com or +1 (888) 901-7776

Dedicated to my beautiful and creative granddaughter, Ellie. You and Alexander are my inspiration.

Alexander woke up from a cat nap when he heard the voices.

He found himself in a special place called a shelter – a safe place for dogs and cats without a home.

He lived with his mom, brother, and sister on a farm, but not for long.

The kind Mr. and Mrs. Fremont, who took care of them, were getting old and wanted to move.

They were going to a little house near their son and decided to bring his mom along.

The kittens, though, were going to a
shelter where nice people would help
them find new homes.

Many people at the shelter were there to feed and take care of the animals, but Alexander's favorite was Jim.

Jim always took the time to talk to them and give gentle pets.

At the shelter, there were many other cats –

black cats

white cats

orange cats

striped cats

even calico cats!

Alexander's sister and brother were both gray.

Alexander was gray too, but he had a special white patch around one eye, and his ears were quite big.

Sometimes, his sister and brother playfully teased him about his big ears.

Ever since Alexander joined the shelter, many cats found new homes.

One day, a kind lady visited and glanced at all the cats.

When she reached Alexander, his brother, and sister, she remarked,

"No gray cats; they seem too ordinary."

Pointing at Alexander, she giggled,

"And this kitten looks funny with his white patch and big ears!"

In the end, she picked a calico kitten.

On another day, a boy and his parents visited and checked out all the cats.

When they reached Alexander, his brother, and sister, the boy declared,

"Not a gray cat. I want a black cat."

Pointing at Alexander, he laughed,

"That one looks funny with his white
patch and big ears."

In the end, he chose a
black cat with long fur.

The next day, a couple visited Jim and said they wanted two kittens who were brother and sister.

Jim introduced them to Alexander his brother, and his sister.

The couple held them, examining each one closely.

Pointing at Alexander, they chuckled,

"He looks funny with that white patch and big ears. We'll take these other two."

So, they brought Alexander's brother and sister to their new home.

Even with lots of cat friends around, Alexander felt lonely and sad. He thought no one liked his big ears.

One day, Alexander heard Jim enter with a girl named Ellie.

Ellie mentioned she was searching for the perfect cat to be her friend.

She looked at a black cat and said,
"No, not that one."

She glanced at an
orange cat and said,

"No, not that one."

She observed a white cat
with long fur and said,

"No, not that one."

She checked each cat, one by one, and each time she shook her head, saying,

"No, not that one."

At last, Ellie reached Alexander.
With a huge smile, she lifted him up and declared,

"This is the one! He has a cool white eye patch,
and I love his ears!"

"He is perfect! Alexander, you are coming home with me, and we will be best friends!"

Ellie promised Jim that she would love Alexander and take good care of him.

So, Alexander happily left with Ellie to his new home.
He was filled with joy, knowing that he and Ellie would
be best friends forever.

to be continued...

About the Author

Though Alexander Finds A Home marks her first published work, Vicky Ann Meier already has more adventures planned for beloved character Alexander. When not writing from her home in Indiana, Vicky continues her work in the senior living field. She enjoys time with family, walking, and road trips with her beloved dog Mikey. Her children's books share themes of friendship, responsibility, and spreading everyday kindness.

About the illustrator

Mentari enjoys creating illustrations with whimsical, vintage pencil effects that bring beautiful childhood memories.